Worn Path Beneath the Stars

Zara Bernal

BookLeaf Publishing

Presentation by *BookLeaf Publishing*

Web: www.bookleafpub.com

E-mail: info@bookleafpub.com

ISBN : 9789357699341

First edition 2022

DEDICATION

To my Heavenly Father above. May this book glorify you.

ACKNOWLEDGEMENT

To My sisters Alex and Ella, who have helped me through so much, and have always been there for me, even when I took them for granted. To every poet and dreamer. To every person I have run into that felt led to share a part of their testimony. To every person I ever allowed myself to call friend, and to those who I mistakenly called my enemy. You have inspired and helped write these words.

PREFACE

Dear Reader,

There are a couple things you need to know about the writings in this book.

1. Those who are written into these pages -whether they were proxies for the idea or the words are actually about them- those whose hearts met mine in this time of life, don't know that their faces are forever printed on my mind, and written on my heart like the words on these pages.

2. This is not just about me. It was never meant to be about me. Reader, you must understand that we come across people everyday that might need, not just a kind word, but a loving hand, a caring heart. They might need God that day.

So the words written into this book, however unskilled they might be, are for the people who need that kind word of understanding, Who need a person to look at their situation and say, I know what that is like. They are for the person needing God today. Let me relate to you, dear Reader, Allow me, if only for a moment, to look at your life and say, I have been there, and look, by God's grace I am here too.

Wanderer Travel earths lawn

Cool winds blow on
Hearing sights seeing sounds
Wanderer travel earths lawn

As I walk and it does darken
I hear rain as it resounds
Cool wind blows on

I am passing on and on
Beautiful howl of walking hounds
Wanderer travel earths lawn

God has created, no other can
I look at it all my heart pounds
Cool winds blow on

Light that grows in dark upon
Through creation God's glory abounds
Cool winds blow on
Wanderer traveling earths lawn

Complete Stranger

His hands and arms were firm
Holding me closer than a friend
Dancing to a tune with our ears
Understanding the steps with our feet
He directed those steps
He controlled those motions
Across the dance floor, I followed
And I trusted him completely

Simple Things

It was the simple things then
Running through snow
Pleasures that seemed small
But were the best to a child

Crouching under a bush
Giggling while others
Ran by not knowing
You were sitting there giggling

It was the simple things then
Playing in gardens
Joys that adults don't know
But were treasures to a child

Climbing to the highest point
Through the autumn leaves
Feeling the wind
And laughing with it
It was the simple things then
Laughing singing shouting
Things no one will grasp
But are all that's needed for a child

Strings tied by God

Sometimes it's sitting
Quiet in a loud room
Staring off spacing out
Moments of stillness

Sometimes it's wondering
How God tied these strings
Of strangers of friends
That now they are family

You are

You bridal joy like a show horse
And display it proudly in your eyes

Your strength is in your character
Carried strongly on a bed of beauty

How do you love?

Do you hold their heart
Like you hold their hand?
Don't squeeze too tight
Don't let it go
Love it while you can
Because one day
It may be gone
The bond we share
The hands we hold
Telling stories of our journey
Remembering the good the bad
But time holds all the memories

-If i could paint-

If i could paint
My subject would be you
I'd make your eyes green
And show a light
That others can't see

If I could paint
The colors of the sunset
Would be your smile
And your hands
Would be a warm beach

If I could paint
I'd find a color
To represent your smell
Like a warm burgundy
Or a soft autumn red

If I could paint
I'd paint your care
A rosy pink
And your laugh a sunset Gold

I wish I could paint
So my subject would be you
And the world could see

All the colors I see
in you

Then you

I used to hate mirrors
Pictures, my reflection,
showing myself
I used to cover up
Hidden behind my masks
of clay and solitude
I said I'm fine
lying to save face I
Closed all the doors
to hide my soul
So No one could touch me

Then you smiled And laughed
Your heart set there
Placed in your eyes
Why I would need to hide
You didn't know
So you watched and listened
Attentive to every word
You saw my soul, hidden
Coaxing it out
So you could see its truth
Understanding its voice

Desire of my heart

Hold me like you love me
Like you'll never let me go
Kiss me like you'd miss
All the kisses after i'm gone
Love me like you've known me
All the days of my life
Whisper to me futures
And what they'll bring us
Because no matter what
In your words you'd stay
And you'd hold me like you love me
For the rest of our days

Ours

A park bench
A kiss sent
A long talk filled with laughs

A car seat
A heartbeat
A head lays on my lap

A firefly
A night sky
A walk among the stars

A whisper
A giggle
And all of it is ours

Two are better

Two are better
One picks up the other
Two speak and share truth when
One cannot escape their thoughts
Two can carry more than
One which is burdened easily
Two and more help encourage when
One loses their way
Two are better than one

Us

We stared into mirrors
And danced in living rooms
Your sister laughed when I fell off your couch

We kissed on playgrounds
In parking lots
Under street lights

We argued in cars
Behind phones
With our backs to each other

We cried in our arms
Behind text messages
And under blankets

We forgave with a hug
A smile on a park bench
A tear in your van
And a kiss on the forehead

Love is...

A fresh pot of coffee in the early morning air
Breakfast in bed made by your favorite person
A toasty blanket fresh from the dryer
Fire-orange leaves falling in the autumn air
When you just need that one person, and they show up
Quiet nights with a hot drink and a really good book
A long drive down a winding country road
Watching stars from atop a hill
Someone to light your way when you're too scared to move in the dark
Someone calling your name from a distance

All your words

Repeating in my head
Like a sweet melody
Where are you now?
Where is that sweet voice?
Music long gone
Melodies never to be heard
Felt only in my dreams
Feelings slowly fading
Dreams slowly dying
Music disappearing
Ears going deaf
Hands going numb
Breath heaving sighs
Eventually going quiet

Empty

Empty
Promises whispered over distance
Secrets spoken in the dark of night
Now I understand the phrase sweet nothings
Every seam you ripped You tried to repair
Only to have taken apart your work
And then some

Send Me Away

Send me away
Send me far far away
Where the pain is left in the town,
And the memories are a distant sound
Send me away

Send me away
To a different home
Where different family hold me close
Where smiles come from new faces
And family has a new meaning
Send me away

Send me far away
Where pain and sadness leave my heart
Where you are the only face I see
Where your glory shines in majesty
And you are the only one for me
Send me away

Endings

Whisping thoughts
Catch fire memories
Burning around me
I call beyond
But the echo never returned
Closing doors
New sounds rise
Silencing their own tune

Behind His Eyes

He was angry
I heard him cry
Middle of the night
Terror behind his eyes
But He didn't speak
He wouldn't dare
To open his mouth
Was far worse
Than what stood
Behind his eyes

He didn't see I was there
He didn't hear me call his name
He couldn't understand the words

So I watched
Prayed as he cried
Middle of the night
Praying hed see
Hoping he'd know
To open his mouth
Was far better
Than listening
To the sounds
Behind his eyes

Desperate Prayer

To be shot down by my own thoughts,
And buried below marsh anger and clay jealousy,
But although my wings fail Catch me,
Catch me on clouds of your mercy,
Lift me above the ground on wings of your forgiveness,
And rest me under the tree of your love,
When I'm tripping over my shame,
Guide my steps with your wisdom,

Wish you were here

Time will stop, and wave, as you hold your
breath
You remember why you will miss them most
You watch it take hold, and last of all death
'Remember' you say, of everything
When they held you close and you watched
them fly
They made you coffee and watched when you'd
sing
They held you on nights when you could not try
You know why they held you, before and now
You wished you had held them tighter before
Now they are gone on the wind like a dove
But you know the reason they stayed was love

New Dawn

Before the dawn a trace of light
Time holds its breath, frozen, calm
Which morning releases into the quiet
Chasing away the last of the dark
Slicing through shadow colors resound
Welcome the delicate chaos

Welcome the delicate chaos
Tickle of wind, laughter of light
The cold of the night loses its resound
To the golden caress that calms
Twirling away from the monotonous dark
A deliberate refusal of quiet

A deliberate refusal of quiet
The vibrant shades painting chaos
Nip the heels of the monsters out of the dark
Life grasps at time enticing light
To favor calamity over calm
Let alive resound

Let alive resound
Burn away the quiet
Savor the absence of calm
Embrace the steady chaos
The unbearable light
An unprepared dive into mury dark

An unprepared dive into murky dark
Breath stolen by the jolting winds resound
Grey clouds, the once so present light
Through evenings chorus, newfound quiet
Even in the eruption of twilights chaos
Feel an accustomed calm

Feel an accustomed calm
Assurance of approaching dark
Reflecting on the beautiful chaos
Colors give way to shadow’s gentle resound
Surrender to quiet
Dusk released a last breath to night’s soft light

The waking worlds chaos fades to joyous calm,
The moon’s light dances with dark,
Echoes of life's final resound until new dawn
breaks the quiet

www.ingramcontent.com/pod-product-compliance
Lightning Source LLC
Chambersburg PA
CBHW051755130826
49812CB00033B/1169
9789357699341